Unplug to Recharge

An Adolescent's Guide to Less Screen-Time and Healthier Me-Time

Written and Illustrated by Caitlin Ruhl

Introduction

What This Project Is All About

Hello! My name is Caitlin and I am a Girl Scout Ambassador. For a long time, I have dealt with stress and anxiety, and watched my friends struggle with the same things. That is why I decided to write a book filled with activities that help reduce and handle stress and anxiety for my Girl Scout Gold Award.

While I was researching topics for my book, I decided to focus on just one cause of stress- too much screen time[1]. When used in moderation things such as social media, Netflix, and video games can actually be good stress relievers. However, it is when they are used excessively that they become a problem[2]. In today's world, screens are unavoidable.

---

1 https://www.washingtonpost.com/news/inspired-life/wp/2018/01/22/teens-who-spend-less-time-in-front-of-screens-are-happier-up-to-a-point-new-research-shows/?noredirect=on&utm_term=.d6f98703bed0 New research shows teens who spend less time in front of screens are less stressed.
2 https://www.ncbi.nlm.nih.gov/pubmed/30406005?smid=nytcore-ios-share There are associations between excessive screen time and lower psychological well-being in adolescents.

We use them for everything from communicating with friends and family to doing research for school. In fact, I used the internet and screens a lot while working on my project! The trick is knowing how to manage and limit your screen time. Like most things, screens are perfectly good in small doses. It is always important to be aware of how long you use screens, and to be sure you set a limit. Not sure how to do this? Don't worry! I will show you plenty of management and moderation tips in the following sections.

In this book, I will give you lots of alternative activities and ways to balance screen time. Of course, we're all different and maybe not every activity I suggest works for you. That's OK! Think of this book as a menu; there are a lot of options to choose from, but you don't need to use all of them. In fact, you may come up with some of your own options. Also, this book is a collection of suggestions to help reduce stress caused by excessive screen time, so if you are suffering from extreme stress or anxiety, you might want to look into professional help.

This may include:

1. CentraCare Clinic (specifically their counseling and psychology services) 320-200-3200

2. Village Family Center 1-800-627-8220

3. Processus Counseling 320-252-2976

4. Imagine Chiropractic 320-240-6561

Outdoors

Being outside can help relieve stress

Time and again, it has been said that nature is good for your health and not just your physical, but mental health, too. If ever you feel like you've been cooped up inside for too long and you can feel the stress mounting, take a break and step outside. Almost immediately, you will begin to calm down. How does this happen? How can something as simple as taking a walk be such a surefire way to reduce anxiety? Allow me to explain.

On the simplest level, nature relaxes the mind, reducing stress and anxiety in the process. Dig a little deeper and you will begin to see why. Stress hormones, such as cortisol, are reduced by exposure to nature. Not only that, but "experiencing nature increases the activity of the parasympathetic nervous system, the part of the nervous system responsible for digestion and rest; part of its activity involves slowing the heart rate. When the parasympathetic nervous system is active, physical side effects of anxiety decrease and subjective feelings of peace and relaxation increase."[3] It's not just the science that supports this fact, the stats do too. In a study conducted by British Military Fitness, they found that of the 1,000 people surveyed, 53.3 percent reported feeling better after being outdoors, and thirty-five percent said that their mood was boosted after exercise.[4]

While simply sitting out of doors is technically a good way to relieve stress, the best way to relieve stress is by participating in an outdoor activity. Below I have listed a few ideas that cover a whole range of outdoor activities:

1. Visit a local park. If you're able, try to find a State or National Park. They're great for hiking, camping, biking, and all sorts of nature fun!

2. Chill beside (or in!) a body of water. Nothing beats a good old fashioned Minnesota lake day.

3. Go to an outdoor concert. Support local artists and spend time outside? What's better than that?

4. Go to the carnival. Mini donuts...Yum!

5. Visit local gardens. Don't have any? Start your own!

(See Green Thumb)

6. Go sledding. Even the dead of winter can't stop you from getting outdoors.

7. Build a snowman, or even a whole snow family!

8. If it's autumn, you can rake the fallen leaves into a pile and jump!

9. Spot clouds on a windy day. Bring a friend and try to spot the wackiest shapes.

Run-a-Ton

Turning exercise into a coping mechanism for anxiety

Exercise is a great next step in reducing stress and anxiety. Not only does it improve your physical health, but your mental health as well. Studies show that when you exercise you reduce fatigue, improve alertness and concentration, and enhance overall cognitive function. Much like exercise, stress affects both your physical and mental health, just in a negative way.

The brain is full of nerve connections, which means that when it is affected by stress and anxiety the rest of the body is impacted as well. Physical activities, such as running, dancing, and any exercise, produce endorphins. Endorphins work as your own natural painkillers, and also improve your ability to sleep (which is another great way to reduce stress). When you're feeling overwhelmed with stress and anxiety, prescribe yourself a workout of low to moderate intensity, and immediately start to feel the endorphins

pumping[5].

Not sure where to start? Don't worry. I've found some

great workout ideas that can be mastered by even the

couchiest of potatoes.

---

5 https://adaa.org/understanding-anxiety/related-illnesses/other-related-conditions/
stress/physical-activity-reduces-st Physical activity reduces stress.

1. Turn on some music and Just Dance!

2. A simple, daily workout of 30 sit-ups, 30 push-ups, and a 30 minutes walk or jog is an excellent way to start of your day.

3. Joining a sport, whether it be from tennis to swimming, or from soccer to hockey, is a wonderful way to not only get in the exercise you need, but also to make friends along the way.

4. Join a gym. It might sound frightening, but gyms such as the YMCA offer interesting and unusual classes, such as rock climbing or tae kwon do, that you might not try otherwise.

5. Yoga! But more on that later...

Deep Breathes

A few breathing exercises and how they can improve stress and anxiety.

Anxiety and stress, when built up, can become difficult to deal with. Sometimes, those pent up emotions become overwhelming to the point of distraction. Everyone deals with this overflow of emotion in different ways, but deep breathing is something anyone can practice, and at any time. Whether you're alone in your room, in a classroom full of people, sitting for an important test, about to give a speech, or any other situation where the anxiety becomes unbearable, deep, slow breathing is an excellent way to quietly take a step back, focus, and calm yourself down.

It's strange to think that something as simple as breathing can help ease anxiety but it's true! The science behind it is simple; when you focus on your breathing technique, you automatically slow your heart rate. The positive effect on your anxiety is almost instantaneous![6]

_____

6 https://www.psychologytoday.com/us/blog/in-practice/201607/breathing-techniques-anxiety Breathing techniques can help anxiety.

Breathing properly may seem pretty straightforward. After all, you do it all the time. However, there are some breathing techniques that require focus and practice to perfect. They are more than just your normal breathing, and that is why they are so effective against stress and anxiety. Below, I've listed two easy breathing strategies as well as an explanation on how to correctly practice them. Let's get started...and don't forget- just breathe!

Belly Breathing: This technique is fairly simple. All you have to do is breathe out. Really focus on the exhale, making sure that all of the air is out of your lungs before you start to inhale. In fact, your in-breath will naturally lengthen with your out-breath, so only focus on the exhale. When you breathe out, try to make it slow, steady and gentle. Focus more on being slow than on being deep. With all this in mind, here are the steps:

1. Breathe in through your nose and let your belly swell with air.

2. Breathe out through your nose.

3. Place one hand on your belly, and one hand on your

chest.

4. As you breathe in, feel your belly rise. As you breathe out, feel your belly lower[7].

Lion's Breath: For this technique, remember all the same tips from belly breathing. Really focus on slow, steady breaths, but also try to get as deep as you can. For this exercise, it helps if you imagine yourself as a lion. Open your mouth wide and let out all your breath.

1. Breathe in through your nose and let your belly fill with air.

2. When you can't breathe in any more, let out all your air through a wide, open mouth. Breathe out with a slight "Ahh" sound.

3. Repeat several times.

---

7 https://www.webmd.com/balance/stress-management/stress-relief-breathing-techniques#1 Deep breathing exercises that help with anxiety.

Green Thumb

Plants and their ability to improve your mood

Nature is good for anxiety; that idea has been proven by scores of scientists. However, experiencing nature isn't always an option for everyone. Some people live in large cities where grass is replaced by asphalt. Others live in places where the harsh weather makes going outside unbearable. And there are still others who simply don't have the means to escape into nature. That is where gardens come in. In this section, I will talk about two types of gardens, and their benefits: indoor gardens and outdoor gardens.

Most people agree that growing plants in your house helps to relieve stress[8], but did you know there is a scientific reason for it? When we breath, we release carbon dioxide and absorb oxygen. Plants do the opposite! Having a plant in your house is like having your own little organic air filter. In fact, NASA research shows that houseplants can filter out

---

8 https://www.psychologytoday.com/us/blog/urban-mindfulness/200903/plants-make-you-feel-better Plants in your space can help you feel better.

87 percent of air toxins in just a day![9] The healing power of plants has been recognized for thousands of years and is still applicable in today's technology-driven world. Even if the plants you grow don't technically have any medical properties, the simple act of caring for a living thing can act like a medicine. Caring for plants is therapeutic, and watching them grow, knowing that you were vital in helping this plant stay alive, is soothing. Plants are beautiful, steady, and slow. In other words, everything you need to break the cycle of stress. Here is a list of indoor plants that are easy (and rewarding!) to care for:

1. Jasmine
2. Aloe Vera
3. Pothos
4. Snake Plant
5. English Ivy
6. Marimo

For those with the room, means, and dedication, outdoor gardens can be just the thing to take your mind off

9 https://www.nbcnews.com/better/health/indoor-plants-can-instantly-boost-your-health-happiness-ncna781806) Research shows that houseplants clean the air we breathe.

the worries and troubles of life. Though they are higher maintenance, outdoor gardens have their own unique benefits. First, you get the added bonus of spending time in the fresh air. On top of that, growing your own fruits and vegetables is a great first step to eating healthier (see the next chapter), as well as a way to help the environment! Growing an outdoor garden isn't easy, but with dedication and perseverance, the reward of a lush, thriving garden is worth the toil.[10] Here are some outdoor plants that are known to help relieve stress and anxiety to get you started:[11]

1. Lavender
2. Chamomile
3. Valerian
4. Lemon Balm
5. St. John's Wort
6. Daisies

10 https://greenstategardener.com/can-plants-help-relieve-stress-and-anxiety/ This article offers a more thorough list of plants that help relieve stress.
11 https://www.serenataflowers.com/pollennation/plants-anti-anxiety-benefits/ Here are 8 plants with amazing anti-anxiety benefits.

Bon Appetit

Become a health-savvy eater, and a relaxed one too!

Not only does your diet affect your physical health, but it affects your mental health as well. Drinking plenty of water, almost more than you think you need, is also shown to help with mental health. Studies conducted by Harvard and the Mayo Clinic have proven the benefits of a healthier diet, and in their research they've come up with some basic foods that are shown to help relieve stress and anxiety.

First, eat protein at breakfast, such as eggs or Greek

yogurt. This will help you stay fuller longer, and also keep your blood sugar steady, thus giving you more energy throughout the day. For lunch or dinner, consider carbs. "Carbohydrates are thought to increase the amount of serotonin in your brain, which has a calming effect. Eat foods rich in complex carbohydrates, such as whole grains — for example, oatmeal, quinoa, whole-grain breads and whole-grain cereals. Steer clear of foods that contain simple carbohydrates, such as sugary foods and drinks."[12] You want to try and avoid these foods because eating an excess of them will increase your risk of disease.

As much as I hate to say it, it is also recommended that in order to reduce anxiety, you should avoid excessive amounts of caffeine. It might be hard for some at first, but replacing a cup of coffee in the morning with a mug of steaming hot herbal tea is just the thing to start off a stress free day.

---

12 https://www.mayoclinic.org/diseases-conditions/generalized-anxiety-disorder/expert-answers/coping-with-anxiety/faq-20057987 A balanced and healthy diet can make a difference when it comes to anxiety.

Above all, it is important to eat fresh. In the winter, this can be harder since most fruits and vegetables are out of season. However, fresh and local fruits and vegetables are abundant in the summer, so take advantage of it! Eating a green salad for lunch instead of, say, a frozen pizza, can help reduce stress and anxiety, and promote peace of mind. To start you off, here are some healthy foods and their benefits:

1. For breakfast, eat eggs or oatmeal to fill you up. Eggs are full of protein and will boost your blood sugar, while oatmeal is a complex carbohydrate and will calm you down. Instead of coffee, try drinking a cup of herbal tea! They come in all sorts of fun, interesting flavours such as rose or ginger.

2. At lunchtime, try something light, such as a fresh salad or fish. As a side, perhaps you could have a bowl of fruit picked fresh from your garden! This type of meal will keep you full and healthy.

3. Finally, for dinner, try a classic such as wild rice soup

with a side of broccoli. To add a little something sweet, try a dish of cherries![13] Carbohydrates and vegetables? What a way to end a day!

13 https://www.mayoclinic.org/diseases-conditions/generalized-anxiety-disorder/expert-answers/coping-with-anxiety/faq-20057987 Nutritional strategies to ease anxiety.

Bake Like a Pro

Three easy recipes that can be mastered even by beginners.

While eating healthy is an important part of dealing with anxiety, cooking/baking comfort foods is another helpful way to relieve stress. While you're cooking, you become immersed in the recipe and distracted from your problems. Not only that, but at the end you get the reward of a delicious treat! Think you're not skilled enough to bake? Don't worry, you don't have to be a professional to cook up a storm! Below are some simple recipes that are both easy and delicious.

London Fog[14] Total Time: 5 minutes *Yield: 1 mug*

INGREDIENTS:

- 1 Earl Grey tea bag
- ½ cup hot water
- ½ cup unsweetened vanilla almond milk (or other milk of choice)
- ¼ tsp vanilla extract
- 1–2 tsp raw honey, maple syrup or sweetener of choice

---

14 https://www.thehealthymaven.com/how-to-make-a-london-fog How to make a steamy cup of London Fog.

INSTRUCTIONS:

1. Steep your tea bag in hot water for 3-5 mins (depending on strength preference)

2. Mix together almond milk and vanilla extract and steam or froth depending on what tools you have.*

3. Stir sweetener in with steeped tea and top with frothed milk.

4. Enjoy hot!

NOTES* If you don't have a frother, heat up milk on stove top. It won't get foamy but it does the trick!

Classic Baked Mac N Cheese[15] Total time: 47 minutes

Serves: 6-8

INGREDIENTS:

- 2 cups milk

- 2 tablespoons butter

- 2 tablespoons all-purpose flour

- ½ teaspoon salt

- ¼ teaspoon freshly ground black pepper

- 1 (10-oz.) block extra sharp Cheddar cheese, shredded

- ¼ teaspoon ground pepper (optional)

- ½ package elbow macaroni. Cooked.

---

15 https://www.southernliving.com/recipes/classic-baked-macaroni-and-cheese-recipe
How to make maccaroni and cheese.

INSTRUCTIONS:

1. Preheat oven to 400°. Microwave milk at HIGH for 1 1/2 minutes. Melt butter in a large skillet or Dutch oven over medium-low heat; whisk in flour until smooth. Cook, whisking constantly, 1 minute.

2. Gradually whisk in warm milk, and cook, whisking constantly, 5 minutes or until thickened.

3. Whisk in salt, black pepper, 1 cup shredded cheese, and, if desired, red pepper until smooth; stir in pasta. Spoon pasta mixture into a lightly greased 2-qt. baking dish; top with remaining cheese. Bake at 400° for 20 minutes or until golden and bubbly.

Chocolate Chip Cookies[16]

INGREDIENTS:
- 8 tablespoons of salted butter
- 1/2 cup white sugar (I like to use raw cane sugar with a coarser texture)
- 1/4 cup packed light brown sugar

---

16 https://pinchofyum.com/the-best-soft-chocolate-chip-cookies How to make chocolate chip cookies.

- 1 teaspoon vanilla
- 1 egg
- 1 1/2 cups all purpose flour (more as needed – see video)
- 1/2 teaspoon baking soda
- 1/4 teaspoon salt (but I always add a little extra)
- 3/4 cup chocolate chips (I use a combination of chocolate chips and chocolate chunks)

INSTRUCTIONS:

1. Preheat the oven to 350 degrees. Microwave butter for about 40 seconds to just barely melt it. It shouldn't be hot – but it should be almost entirely in liquid form.

2. Using a stand mixer or electric beaters, beat the butter with the sugars until creamy. Add the vanilla and the egg; beat on low speed until just incorporated – 10-15 seconds or so (if you beat the egg for too long, the cookies will be stiff).

3. Add the flour, baking soda, and salt. Mix until crumbles form. Use your hands to press the crumbles together into a dough. It should form one large ball

that is easy to handle (right at the stage between "wet" dough and "dry" dough). Add the chocolate chips and incorporate with your hands.

4. Roll the dough into 12 large balls (or 9 for HUGELY awesome cookies) and place on a cookie sheet. Bake for 9-11 minutes until the cookies look puffy and dry and just barely golden.Warning, friends: DO NOT OVERBAKE. This advice is probably written on every cookie recipe everywhere, but this is essential for keeping the cookies soft. Take them out even if they look like they're not done yet (see picture in the post). They'll be pale and puffy.

5. Let them cool on the pan for a good 30 minutes or so (I mean, okay, eat four or five but then let the rest of them cool). They will sink down and turn into these dense, buttery, soft cookies that are the best in all the land.

Perfect Pose

Yoga poses for the novice and how they help with stress

Did you know yoga can help relieve stress and anxiety?

It's true! In ancient times, yoga was practiced by those who wished to gain enlightenment and become one with the universe. Nowadays, many people use it to calm their hectic and stressful lives. Yoga is a mind-body practice.[17] Put simply, this means that practicing yoga involves a combination of physical poses, controlled breathing (which we covered in the Deep Breathes chapter), and purposeful thinking or meditation (which we will cover in a later

17 https://www.mayoclinic.org/healthy-lifestyle/stress-management/in-depth/yoga/art-20044733 Yoga helps to fight stress and find peace in your life.

chapter). Through this combination, your muscles relax, heart rate lowers, and so does your blood pressure. All of these effects help to lower stress and reduce anxiety. And do you want to know the best thing about yoga? Anyone can do it! All you need is a mat and a little bit of free time, and you're aboard the train to the relaxation station. For those interested, yoga classes are often offered at gyms such as the YMCA, or at local yoga studios. However, for those who might not have the time, means, or interest in a class, Youtube is a great resource. Just search for yoga and you'll have thousands of different videos to choose from.

Here are five easy yoga poses to get you started on your yoga journey:

1. **Bridge Pose:** Lay with your back on the ground, arms to the side with your palms up. Slowly raise your hips until your knees make a straight line with your shoulders. Hold it until you are settled into it, then focus on clearing your thoughts and steadying your breathing.

2. **Child's Pose:** Kneel on the floor and slowly lean forward as far as you can. Try to touch your forehead to the ground. Breath out as you are doing this and slowly reach your arms out in front of you, stretching them as far as they will go. Once again, hold the pose and focus on your thoughts and breathing.

3. **Cat Pose:** For this pose, kneel on the ground on all fours. Make sure your arms are in line with your legs, and that your hands are no wider than your shoulders, and your knees no wider than your hips. From there, arch your back up as far as it will go, then hold. Alternate this pose with the cow pose, always going slowly and focus on your breathing.

4. **Cow Pose:** Start the same way you did for the cat pose, only this time instead of arching your back, dip it down as deep as it will go. Alternate slowly with the cat pose.

5. **Triangle Pose:** This pose is the most difficult of

the five, but don't worry. Just go slowly and stop wherever you feel you need to. Start by standing straight up, then slowly widen your stance. As you widen your legs, turn your torso so that your left arm reaches for your left foot. Stop when they meet. Your torso should be parallel to the floor at that point. Now, open up your torso by slowly rotating your right arm up towards the sky until it is straight up and down. Hold this pose, then slowly rewind and do it again on the other side.

Bookworm

Feeling overwhelmed? Curl up with one of these classic books!

Instead of picking up a screen to fill your empty hours,

try picking up a book- particularly if you've been feeling

anxious or stressed. Reading is a great way to escape

from the stresses of everyday life[18] and instead go on an

---

18 https://www.bustle.com/p/5-ways-reading-can-help-you-cope-with-anxiety-57431
Differnt was that books help ease stress.

incredible adventure; and maybe even learn a thing or two along the way. Not only that, but recent studies have shown that reading a good story can actually increase our compassion for another's suffering-as well as to our own. This can lead to self-growth and healing and eventually to a decrease in stress and anxiety.[19] Today, with the world at our fingertips, it is easy to pick up a screen and escape into the convoluted world of social media. You might think that doing so isn't much different than escaping into a good book. In fact, while social media might not be the cause of all stress and anxiety, it definitely works to increase and escalate existing stresses. Books, on the other hand, help you to see outside yourself and focus, two traits that are key to soothing an anxious mind.[20]

---

19 https://psychcentral.com/blog/why-novel-reading-reduces-anxiety/ Novel reading can help reduce anxiety.
20 https://www.healthyplace.com/blogs/anxiety-schmanxiety/2016/04/anxiety-and-reading-how-reading-has-helped-me-cope-with-my-anxiety Books help soothe anxious minds.

For those of you who might not know where to start looking for good stories, never fear. I have come up with a list of five books that are considered classics and are sure to be an immersive read.

1. *Anne of Green Gables* By: L.M. Montgomery
   This is the story of a young orphan girl as she grows up, and all of the misadventures she has along the way.

2. *The Lion, the Witch, and the Wardrobe* By: C.S. Lewis
   Follow the Pevensie siblings as they get lost in a wardrobe world full of talking animals, endless winters, evil witches, and a regal lion.

3. *The Hobbit* By: J.R.R.Tolkien
   What happens when thirteen homeless dwarves, an old wizard, and one stubborn hobbit go on an adventure to defeat a dragon? This book will show you!

4. T*he Adventures of Tom Sawyer* By: Mark Twain
   It ain't easy being Tom Sawyer, but having an unwieldy imagination, a quick wit, and a band of loyal friends sure helps. The lure of adventure, robbers, and treasure doesn't hurt, either.

5. *The Westing Game* By: Ellen Raskin
   Riddles, fortunes, families, and mystery all combine to create the page-turning puzzle of the Westing Game.

Furry Friends

Animals and their calming effect.

Did you know that pets, especially cats and dogs, are great at reducing stress and anxiety? That's right! Studies have proven that pets reduce stress and anxiety, ease loneliness, encourage exercise and playfulness, and even improve your heart's health![21] Simply playing with your pet can increase your levels of serotonin and dopamine, two chemicals that help you to calm down and relax. Over the centuries of human civilization, pets have become an integral part of our lives. They depend on us for food, a place to sleep, and safety. In return, they give us companionship and unconditional love. However, we now know that they give us even more than that: "A 2016 study explored the role of pets in the social networks of people managing a long-term mental health problem and found that pets provide a sense of security and routine that provided emotional and social support. Studies have also

---

21 https://www.helpguide.org/articles/mental-health/mood-boosting-power-of-dogs. htm Pets such as cats and dogs can help relieve stress and anxiety.

shown that pets are facilitators of getting to know people, friendship formation and social support networks."[22]

Your pet doesn't even have to be a cat or a dog in order to help reduce anxiety. Just by watching your fish swim around its aquarium, you reduce muscle tension and lower your heart rate. Don't have a pet? Don't worry! Visiting animal shelters and playing with the animals there is a great substitute for a pet. And, who knows? Maybe you'll leave with a new family member!

22 https://adaa.org/learn-from-us/from-the-experts/blog-posts/consumer/alleviating-anxiety-stress-and-depression-pet How pets relieve our stress and anxiety.

Tuned Out

Music can help reduce anxiety, and a playlist of soothing songs.

Music is universal; it has no borders and no boundaries. Every emotion has a soundtrack to accompany it. If you're happy, there's music to help you stay that way, same if you're feeling sad. But if you're feeling stressed, is there music to help you feel calm? The answer is yes. To put it matter of factly: "Listening to music can have a tremendously relaxing effect on our minds and bodies, especially slow, quiet classical music. This type of music can have a beneficial effect on our physiological functions, slowing the pulse and heart rate, lowering blood pressure, and decreasing the levels of stress hormones. Music, in short, can act as a powerful stress management tool in our lives."[23]

Not only that, but music demands our attention, allowing us to focus on it, and not on whatever is causing our stress or anxiety. There are endless types of music and countless

---

23 https://psychcentral.com/lib/the-power-of-music-to-reduce-stress/ Music can reduce stress and anxiety.

songs for each mood. It is up to you to decide which type is best for you. However, studies have shown that classical music most often works the best for calming anxiety.

Just as there are many different genres of music, there are also many different ways to consume it. You could simply lay on your bed with a pair of headphones and unwind after a long day.[24] Or maybe you prefer to jam in the car on the way home. It's up to you! Not sure where to start looking for calming music? Streaming  stations such as Spotify and Pandora are free, and they are full to the brim with every type of music imaginable! Simply search for calming or soothing music, select a playlist, and start listening. If those can't be reached, try turning on your local classical music radio station and let go of your worries.

24 Https://www.statepress.com/article/2017/09/music-can-help-students-cope-with-the-stress-and-anxiety-of-being-in-college How music reduces stress and anxiety.

Best Dressed

Dressing comfortably and in your own style can help with identity anxiety.

Believe it or not, everyone has style. The key to rocking that style is finding one that makes you comfortable. Try things out and experiment! Find a style that embodies and emboldens you. Nowadays, it is easy to get bombarded by the ever changing trends of fashion. It may seem that as soon as you finally buy that pair of expensive hightops, the trends move on and suddenly sandals are the "must-have" item. If following fashion trends and staying up-to-date is what makes you happy then by all means, do it! But if it's not your thing, that's fine too!

Your value as a person doesn't hinge on whether or not you bought that expensive designer coat. However, finding a style that you are comfortable in (whatever style that may be) is an important part of gaining confidence in yourself. By doing so, you can lift some of that stress and anxiety off of your fashionable shoulders! Not sure where to start? One great-and cheap- place to find cool clothes is your local thrift shop!

Artist's Touch

Art can aid in stressful situations.

Art is a fantastic way to relieve stress and reduce

anxiety. You don't have to create a masterpiece every time

in order for art to help, all you have to do is leave it all on

the page. Art is about expressing how you feel in ways

that you can't put into words, but it's also as simple as just

letting go. You don't have to know what you're creating,

or how you're going to get there, you just have to get it

out and off your chest. Studies have shown that creating art can help with more than just stress relief. It can also alleviate pain, promote wellness, enhance memory, improve communications, aid physical rehabilitation, and give people a way to express their feelings.[25]

One extremely easy way to do this is to buy a coloring book and get to work. It could be a fairly straightforward one, or a complex maze of line and design, or one that falls somewhere in the middle. Whichever style of coloring book you go for, becoming absorbed in filling it in will help relieve some of your stress. If you prefer something a little more in depth than a coloring book, below are some activities recommended by art therapists:

Jackson Pollock inspired art: Get a large, blank sheet of paper, large pots of paint, and a few paintbrushes. Then, begin to splatter the paint all across the canvas. Chuck it, whip it, smear it, even use your fingers if you want!

_____

25 https://www.usatoday.com/story/news/politics/2018/03/22/whether-its-art-and-music-therapy-art-and-music-therapy-calms-traumatized-teens/446622002/ Art therapy helps relieve anxiety.

Make Jackson Pollock proud by splattering that paint as passionately as possible. *Sidenote: this activity is best if done outdoors to reduce the mess.

Altered Magazine Photo: Think of this as defacing a photo. It can be both therapeutic, as well as humorous, and to top it off, there are no drawing or painting skills required! All you need is a page from a magazine, some oil pastels, and maybe some acrylic paint. Then, you alter! Feel free to go as heavy-handed as possible and try to make the page unrecognizable!

Tin Foil Sculpture: This one is pretty self-explanatory. All you need is a roll of tin foil. Set a timer for an hour and see what you can create![26]

26 https://www.expressiveartworkshops.com/how-to-start-your-own-art-program/ spontaneous-art-therapy-activities-for-teens/ Here are some ideas of art projects that help ease stress.

Good and Bad Garbage

Taking out the garbage

In this section, I will talk about two types of garbage: good and bad. "Good garbage" is also known as verbal garbage, while "bad garbage" is physical garbage. Verbal garbage is a great technique for when your head becomes too full with stuff and you need to get it all out. Pick up a pen and just go for it. Write everything down, it doesn't have to make sense, and it doesn't have to be eloquent or poetic. It just has to be let out. Once all the words are out, get up and walk away. Maybe do some exercises from this book and then come back. Take a look at what you wrote and see if you still feel the same way. Practicing this verbal garbage will help clear your head of too much noise, and make it easier to focus on the important things.

The flip side of good garbage is, of course, bad garbage. Bad garbage is when your space (whether it be a room, chair, desk, or nook) becomes cluttered and disorganized. This sort of chaos mimics what is going on in your head. A messy space is a messy mind. The idea is the same as with verbal garbage: get rid of all the excess junk so that only the important things remain. This could mean anything as simple as reorganizing your desk, to as complex as rearranging your room. With all the noise cleared away, it becomes easy to focus on what is causing you to be stressed and anxious, and then to deal with the problem. However, maybe you are the type of person who thrives in this sort of chaos. If so, then keep doing it! If you have a method that works, stick to it. This is merely one suggestion out of many on ways to ease stress and anxiety. After all, there might be a method to your madness!

Inner Peace

Meditation practices and their history of easing anxiety

Meditation is a very, very old practice. The first recorded practice of meditation was in India, dated at around 5000-3500 B.C. This record is wall art depicting people sitting in the cross-legged position with eyes half closed. Meditation began in the Hindu religion and has since spread across the globe to be used by people of all races, religions, creeds, and beliefs. For thousands of years, meditation was used to calm the mind, contemplate existence, and deepen understanding of the sacred and mystical forces of life. Now, studies have shown that meditation can give you a sense of calm, peace, and balance that can benefit both your emotional well-being, as well as your overall health.[27] While those are all great benefits of meditation, one of its best assets is that meditation can be practiced practically anywhere. Whether you are on a bus, in class, taking a test, on a walk, or waiting at the dentist's office, you can practice meditation.

---

27 https://www.mayoclinic.org/tests-procedures/meditation/in-depth/meditation/art-20045858 Meditation eases stress and anxiety.

Meditation is simple, free, and doesn't require any special equipment. Below, I will give you an easy way to practice meditation.

Short meditation: This includes getting in touch with your body and your breathing. Feel your breath as it goes in, and as it goes out. Be aware of your belly rising and falling with each inhale, and with each exhale. Wandering minds should be gently brought back to the meditation, focus on your breath and feel it come in and go out. Inhale through your nose, exhale through your mouth, over and over, in and out. Be sure to sit comfortably, but stay aware of your posture. Feel your body all the way from your crown to your toes, taking stock of any pain, sensation, or emotion. There is no good or bad, just feel it, then let go. Return to your breathing as it comes in and out. Try this for five, maybe ten minutes when you're feeling particularly stressed or anxious, but it can also be used casually to start and end your day.[28]

28 Biegel, Gina M. The Stress Reduction Workbook for Teens: Mindfulness Skills to Help You Deal with Stress. Instant Help Books, 2017

Stay Strong

Focusing on personal strengths, building confidence, and reducing stress.

Have you ever heard the phrase "jack of all trades"?

If not, it basically means doing a little bit of everything.

While that may seem like a good thing, in reality... not

so much. While it is true that we have to do all sorts of

different things everyday, like read, do math, mow the lawn,

take care of siblings, and many more, it is important that

you do not stretch yourself too thin. Now, I'm not saying don't do your chores. What I mean is that when it comes to extracurriculars, like sports and clubs, don't try to do everything. The urge we have to be the best at everything is not only impossible, it is also unhealthy. Find out what you're good at. Maybe it's chess, maybe basketball, maybe you're really, really good at water polo. Who knows! The point is, find your passion and stick to it! By focusing on your strengths instead of fixating on being perfect at everything, you can actually get rid of some of that worry! However, it is also important to remember that you don't have to stick with something if you don't love it anymore, even if you've been doing it for a long time. This is about finding your passion and having fun. If you don't feel that with your activity or hobby, don't be afraid to say no! And remember, even if you're not perfect at something at the first try, stick with it. After all, as Muhammad Ali once said, "even the greatest was once a beginner." Don't be afraid to take that first step.

Seeing is Believing

Visualising yourself ace-ing a stressful situation helps reduce anxiety.

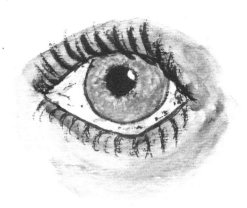

"Practice makes perfect," or at least, that's how the common phrase goes. That phrase is repeated for everything from learning how to juggle to perfecting a synchronized swim routine. However, did you know that it can also be applied to stressful situations? Take a speech for example. Say next week you have to give a speech about bullying in front of your entire class. Even though you're allowed notecards, you're still (rightfully) nervous. Instead of focusing on that fear, try to instead focus on doing everything in your power to prepare. In other words:

practice, practice, practice. Practice your speech in the mirror, on the bus, in front of your family, in front of your dog... you get the idea. The important thing is to become familiar with the speech and the situation. The more comfortable you are, the less nervous you'll be. The main thing to remember is to really visualize yourself not just in the situation, but actually acing it as well. The more you see yourself confidently handling a stressful situation, the more likely it is to come true![29]

And this trick works for any situation that gives you anxiety. Got an interview? Run through any potential questions (as well as any curveballs they might throw) until you can answer them in your sleep. Same goes for upcoming plays, solos, recitals, competitions, games, or meets. Even something as seemingly mundane as answering a question in class can be made easier with visualization. Be as prepared as you possibly can because that is all you can do, and remember, practice makes perfect!

29 https://www.anxietycanada.com/sites/default/files/adult_hmsocial.pdf A few self-help strategies to help with social anxiety.

Treat Yo' Self

Sticks and stones may break your bones, but speaking negatively to yourself heightens anxiety.

One big problem that increases stress and anxiety is negative self-talk. What is negative self-talk? Broadly speaking, it's anything you say to yourself that makes you feel bad. For instance, if you have a big test coming up, negative self-talk would be thinking things like "I'm going to fail" or "I'll never be able to study everything in time." Even if the phrases seem small and insignificant, they each add up to heighten and increase anxiety. Once you start noticing these little snippets, it becomes easier to combat them. As with most issues, step one in finding a solution is identifying the problem. And look, you've just done that! Now, the next step is to actively combat those thoughts with positive, self-affirming thoughts instead. Let's go back to the test example. When you notice yourself thinking those negative thoughts, stop and change the tone. Maybe you'll fail the test, but also maybe not. You might not be able to study everything before the test, but at least you'll have studied something. These sorts of transitional thoughts lead the way toward more positive thinking. Soon, your first thought will be "I'm going to ace the test tomorrow!" instead of "I'm going to fail." With enough practice and enough patience, you'll soon be on your way towards a healthier, more positive mindset. [30]

30 Biegel, Gina M. The Stress Reduction Workbook for Teens: Mindfulness Skills to Help You Deal with Stress. Instant Help Books, 2017.

Higher Power

Strengthening your spiritual beliefs and how they decrease stress.

For millennia, people have found peace, solace, and relief through their religion. No matter what religion it is, whether it be Christianity, Judaism, Islam, Buddhism, Hinduism, Taoism, Sikhism, Confucianism, agnostic spiritualism, or any number of other religions, following and practicing a set of spiritual beliefs is yet another way to help you deal with stress and anxiety. There isn't really a scientific reason as to why religion helps with this, though perhaps in this case there doesn't need to be one. Just knowing that you are not alone, that you are loved, and that you are a part of something bigger than yourself is enough to take away some of the stress from your life. If you're interested, you could take religion a step further by doing some of the following:

1. Attend religious services and worship with fellow believers.

2. Participate in the community in some way. For instance, you could do volunteer work with other people of your faith!

3. Read your religion's holy texts and study the discourse surrounding them.

4. Join a youth group, or if there isn't one already, create one!

Final Steps

Naming the problem, not avoiding difficult conversations, and getting support.

Finally, it is important to remember that all of the tips and strategies in this book are meant to relieve stress and anxiety by being alternatives to screen time. If stress and anxiety continue to be major problems in your life, it might be a good idea to follow these next three steps towards more help:

1. **Naming the Problem:** While it may seem obvious, the first step in dealing with anxiety is naming the problem. By admitting you need help, you open the door to ways of coping and addressing the situation. At first, you only need to name it to yourself. Try things on your own, like the tips in this book or others like it. However, if it is still too much to handle, you might want to bring up the problem with a person you trust, which brings us to the next step.

2. **Don't Avoid Difficult Conversations:** It can be very hard to admit something is wrong, especially to those close to you. Starting a conversation about excessive stress and anxiety is tough, but it only gets harder the longer you wait. However, once you start talking about the problem instead of avoiding it, it becomes easier to handle. Not only that, but odds are you'll find someone who is willing and happy to help you through your difficulties!

3. **Getting Support:** Lastly, it is very important that you get support as you work through your problems. While sometimes it is easier to work alone, it can help to share the weight of what you're dealing with someone you trust. This person could be anyone that you're close with: a parent, sibling, family member, friend, teacher, religious leader, or even counselor. Whoever it happens to be, their role would be one of support and encouragement. They would be there to listen, to guide, to help, to hold you accountable, and

to make sure you're taking the necessary steps to get

better. They will hold your hand through the hard

times, and help share the weight of your difficulties.